DIGGING FOR DINOSAURS

EXCAVATION
EXPLORATION

RACHAEL L. THOMAS

Checkerboard
Library

An Imprint of Abdo Publishing
abdopublishing.com

abdopublishing.com

Published by Abdo Publishing, a division of ABDO, PO Box 398166, Minneapolis, Minnesota 55439. Copyright © 2019 by Abdo Consulting Group, Inc. International copyrights reserved in all countries. No part of this book may be reproduced in any form without written permission from the publisher. Checkerboard Library™ is a trademark and logo of Abdo Publishing.

Printed in the United States of America, North Mankato, Minnesota
052018
092018

Design: Sarah DeYoung, Mighty Media, Inc.
Production: Mighty Media, Inc.
Editor: Megan Borgert-Spaniol
Design elements: Mighty Media, Inc., Shutterstock, Spoon Graphics
Cover photographs: Shutterstock, Spoon Graphics
Interior photographs: Alamy, p. 14 (top left); AP Images, pp. 9 (bottom), 14 (right), 17; Dolly Blue/Flickr, pp. 8, 11; iStockphoto, pp. 4, 25; Jon Austria/The Daily Times/AP Images, p. 23; Shutterstock, pp. 5 (top, bottom), 7, 9 (top), 13, 14 (bottom left), 15, 21, 29; Wikimedia Commons, p. 27

Library of Congress Control Number: 2017961568

Publisher's Cataloging-in-Publication Data
Names: Thomas, Rachael L., author.
Title: Digging for dinosaurs / by Rachael L. Thomas.
Description: Minneapolis, Minnesota : Abdo Publishing, 2019. I Series: Excavation exploration I Includes online resources and index.
Identifiers: ISBN 9781532115233 (lib.bdg.) I ISBN 9781532155956 (ebook)
Subjects: LCSH: Fossils--Juvenile literature. I Dinosaurs--Juvenile literature. I Paleontology--Juvenile literature. I Paleontological excavations--Juvenile literature.
Classification: DDC 567.9--dc23

CONTENTS

PIECES OF
THE PAST

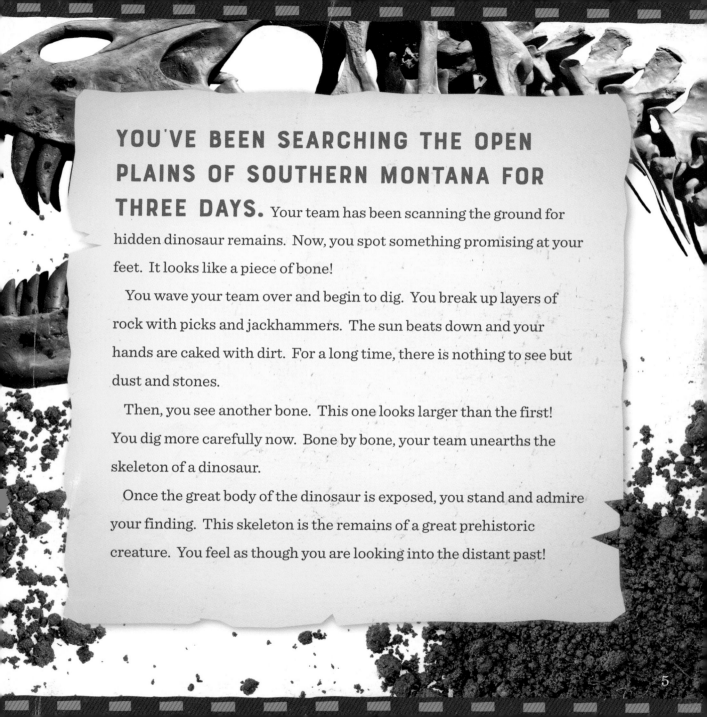

YOU'VE BEEN SEARCHING THE OPEN PLAINS OF SOUTHERN MONTANA FOR THREE DAYS.
Your team has been scanning the ground for hidden dinosaur remains. Now, you spot something promising at your feet. It looks like a piece of bone!

You wave your team over and begin to dig. You break up layers of rock with picks and jackhammers. The sun beats down and your hands are caked with dirt. For a long time, there is nothing to see but dust and stones.

Then, you see another bone. This one looks larger than the first! You dig more carefully now. Bone by bone, your team unearths the skeleton of a dinosaur.

Once the great body of the dinosaur is exposed, you stand and admire your finding. This skeleton is the remains of a great prehistoric creature. You feel as though you are looking into the distant past!

WHAT ARE DINOSAURS?

Dinosaurs are a group of reptiles that first walked Earth around 240 million years ago. They lived during the Mesozoic Era, which ended about 65 million years ago. At this time, an event occurred on Earth that killed many of the planet's species, including dinosaurs.

Scientists are still not certain what event caused this destruction. The most popular theory is that an asteroid hit Earth and covered its surface with ash. The resulting conditions killed plant life as well as many animals that depended on plants. From then on, dinosaurs were extinct.

Today, dinosaur fossils are found in rock all over the world. Paleontologists determine the age of these fossils using radiometric dating. This

DIG THIS!

Over years of research, scientists have learned that dinosaurs were a varied group. The smallest species was the size of a chicken. The largest was nearly as long as three school buses!

method measures the **radioactive** elements in rock containing fossils. This tells researchers how long ago a dinosaur lived.

However, fossil study has taught paleontologists much more than when dinosaurs lived. Fossils reveal what dinosaurs might have looked like and how they might have lived. They also help us better understand the conditions of Earth millions of years before humans walked its surface!

Dinosaurs walked the planet for about 170 million years. That's 850 times longer than modern humans have existed!

TIMELINE

1824

British geologist William Buckland names *Megalosaurus*, the first named dinosaur.

1863

British scientist Thomas Henry Huxley proposes that birds **evolved** from reptiles.

1842

British scientist Richard Owen **classifies** Megalosaurus as a dinosaur.

LATE 1800s – EARLY 1900s

The Great Dinosaur Rush leads to an increase in discoveries of new dinosaur species.

1905
A partial skeleton excavated by Barnum Brown receives the name *Tyrannosaurus rex.*

1996
Scientists discover the fossil imprint of a feathered dinosaur in Liaoning, China.

1979
Jack Horner and his team discover the remains of baby dinosaurs and their nests at Egg Mountain.

2011
Advanced tools allow US paleontologists to excavate delicate dinosaur teeth from sandstone.

MEGALOSAURUS

Humans have likely been finding dinosaur fossils since ancient times. However, they would not have known what creatures the fossils came from. Some scholars believe these finds inspired legends of dragons and other mythical creatures.

Formal study of dinosaurs began about 200 years ago, in the early 1800s. British geologist William Buckland was studying bones that had been found in English **quarries**. In 1824, he decided the fossils came from an animal species that had not been named before. He called the creature *Megalosaurus*.

Megalosaurus was the first named dinosaur. But it wasn't considered a dinosaur until 1842. That year, British scientist

DIG THIS!

When Megalosaurus was named, scientists hadn't yet developed precise fossil dating methods. Instead, scientists could only estimate the relative age of fossils based on the rock layers in which they were found.

Richard Owen **classified** Megalosaurus in a group of prehistoric reptiles he called "Dinosauria."

The study of Megalosaurus fossils marked the rise of a new science. Now, researchers could classify all the amazing fossils being discovered in Britain and beyond. The study of dinosaurs had finally begun!

Only three creatures belonged to Dinosauria when Owen first identified the group. One was Megalosaurus (1). The other two were *Iguanodon* (2) and *Hylaeosaurus* (3).

11

TYRANNOSAURUS REX

By the late 1800s, the search for dinosaur fossils had reached a global scale. It was an era often referred to as the first "Great Dinosaur Rush." Much of this activity took place in North America. Some of the most exciting dinosaur fossil finds in history were discovered in Wyoming, Colorado, Montana, and Canada during this period.

One of these famous finds was discovered in 1902 in a Montana **quarry**. There, American paleontologist Barnum Brown unearthed dinosaur bones unlike any seen before. Brown believed he may have found a new species.

For three years, Brown's team worked to excavate the bones.

DIG THIS!

Dinosaur names have their origins in the Greek and Latin languages. *Tyrannosaurus* means "tyrant lizard" in Greek, and *rex* means "king" in Latin.

The largest and most complete *T. rex* skeleton was discovered in 1990. Nicknamed "Sue," the skeleton is 13 feet (4 m) tall at the hips and 40.5 feet (12 m) long!

They used horse-drawn plows to move layers of soil and rock off the remains. The team also used explosives to blast through hard rock.

In the process, Brown uncovered tail, arm, and jaw bones, as well as teeth. In 1905, the partial skeleton received its now-famous name. It was the *Tyrannosaurus rex*!

BARNUM BROWN

Barnum Brown was born in Carbondale, Kansas, in 1873. His passion for fossil hunting began when he collected fossil shells as a child. As an adult, he worked as a **curator** for the American Museum of Natural History. This job brought him all over the world in search of dinosaur fossils.

Brown was a leader in dinosaur excavation during the Great Dinosaur Rush. He is most famous for his 1902 discovery of *T. rex* fossils. Today, he remains a much-loved figure at the American Museum of Natural History. There, dozens of his discoveries are still on display today!

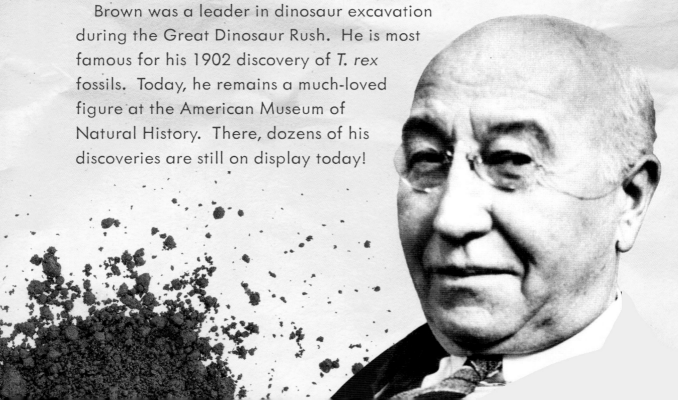

Tyrannosaurus rex, or *T. rex*, fascinated the public. The dinosaur's bones were put on display at the American Museum of Natural History in 1906. Crowds lined up around the block to see the exhibit.

Since Brown's find, many more *T. rex* bones have been found. But Brown's discovery remains famous. It was the first specimen of a new and exciting creature. It would serve as a model for future research on the species!

EGG
MOUNTAIN

The Great Dinosaur Rush slowed down in the late 1930s. By then, dinosaurs were generally viewed as slow-moving, giant lizards. Many people were uninspired by this image and lost interest in the creatures. Dinosaur fossil exploration remained slow through the 1940s and 1950s.

Then, several scientists made new discoveries that changed popular understanding of dinosaurs. American paleontologist John Ostrom published a paper in 1969. He described the discovery of a small, fast-moving, and intelligent dinosaur. This find was one of several that created new excitement for dinosaur fossil discovery.

Ostrom had shown that there were still mysteries to be solved about dinosaurs. One mystery concerned dinosaur babies. By the 1970s, scientists had discovered and excavated many skeletons of adult dinosaurs. But young dinosaur skeletons were almost never found. Fossils of dinosaur babies or dinosaur eggs were even rarer. Scientists wondered why.

Jack Horner helped advise the director of the *Jurassic Park* movies. He also inspired a lead character in the movies, Dr. Alan Grant!

American paleontologist Jack Horner helped solve this mystery. In 1978, he met with a woman named Marion Brandvold. Brandvold owned a rock shop in Bynum, Montana. She showed Horner some fossils she had collected. When Horner saw the bones, he was amazed. Brandvold had a collection of baby dinosaur fossils!

In 1979, Horner and his team began excavating the site where Brandvold had found the fossils. They used shovels and ice picks to dig straight down and remove large chunks of earth. This exposed a clear line where green mudstone changed to red mudstone. By digging out the green mudstone, a bowl-shaped hole was revealed. It was a dinosaur nest!

Over the next few years, Horner's team found 14 fossilized dinosaur nests. Some nests contained the fossilized bones of baby dinosaurs. Other nests held fossilized dinosaur eggs.

Scientists used **CT scans** to produce **3-D** images of the insides of the eggs. This showed that some eggs contained fossilized dinosaur embryos! These were the first embryonic dinosaur skeletons ever found. Horner's discoveries earned the site the name Egg Mountain.

Egg Mountain advanced scientists' understanding of baby dinosaurs. But paleontologists also found adult dinosaur skeletons at the site. This suggested that adult dinosaurs cared for their young after birth. The number of nests found at the site also showed that certain dinosaurs nested in groups. These findings shed light on previously unknown social behaviors of dinosaurs.

EGG MOUNTAIN DINOSAUR NEST

Long ago, a stream flooded the Egg Mountain nests, burying them in sediment. Over time, the bones in the nest turned to fossils.

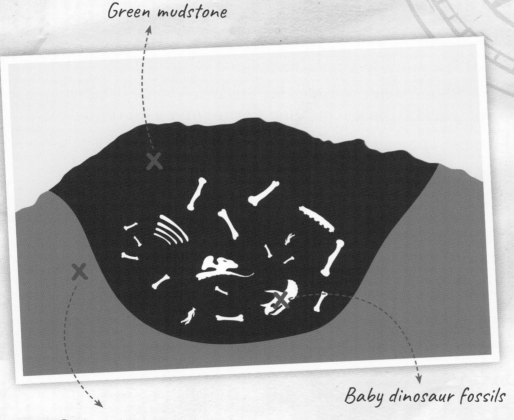

Green mudstone

Red mudstone

Baby dinosaur fossils

SINOSAUROPTERYX

Egg Mountain helped scientists better understand the life cycle of a dinosaur. About twenty years later, a new fossil discovery provided more key information about these animals' existence. It proved a **controversial** theory that dinosaurs **evolved** into birds!

British scientist Thomas Henry Huxley proposed this theory as early as 1863. He pointed out the similarities between reptiles and birds. But few scientists agreed with Huxley. A 1996 discovery changed this.

That year, a team of scientists discovered a dinosaur fossil in the Liaoning region of China. It was an imprint of the dinosaur's body on a slab of rock. The imprint showed a fringe or fur around the outline of the body. This suggested the dinosaur was covered in fuzz-like feathers, as modern birds are.

The dinosaur was named *Sinosauropteryx*. Before its discovery, most scientists assumed all dinosaurs were scaly. Now, it was widely accepted that many dinosaurs had feathers or bristles.

Many more fossils of feathered dinosaurs have since been found in the Liaoning region. These discoveries have persuaded most scientists of the link between dinosaurs and birds. Now, many argue that the birds we see today could be **classified** as reptiles!

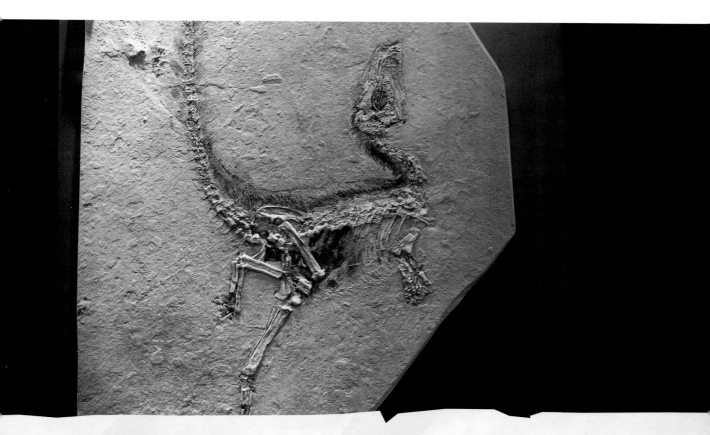

More recent Sinosauropteryx fossil research has revealed clues about the dinosaur's coloring. Researchers think the creature may have had orange feathers and a striped tail.

ADVANCED TOOLS

Methods for locating dinosaur fossils have changed much since the formal study of dinosaurs began. Today's tools allow paleontologists to search for fossils without even breaking the ground! One such tool is called a Geiger counter.

Geiger counters detect **radiation**. Uranium, an element that gives off radiation, is sometimes found in fossilized dinosaur bones. Scientists use Geiger counters to locate this radiation in the ground. Then, researchers can use **X-rays** to examine the bones' structures while the fossils are still underground. This gives scientists a better idea of where and how to dig.

Tools such as shovels, picks, and jackhammers are commonly used to reach a buried fossil. Then, paleontologists remove the fossil with some rock still surrounding it. Before a fossil is taken away from a site, scientists cover it with a casing called a jacket. Jackets protect fossils during transport to labs.

In 2015, a dinosaur fossil was airlifted from its excavation site to a museum in New Mexico. A plaster jacket protected the 4,500-pound (2,041 kg) *Pentaceratops* skull during its helicopter journey.

Jackets are traditionally made of plaster. But recently, some scientists have begun creating jackets using foam. The foam expands perfectly into gaps in the fossil before hardening. Foam jackets are more lightweight than those made of plaster. They can also better absorb bumps and shocks. This makes damage during transport less likely.

After successful transport, researchers work to completely remove the fossil from rock. New tools, such as air scribes, have made this process easier. Air scribes use compressed air to vibrate like drills. They chip away tiny bits of rock from fossils. In 2011, precise tools like these allowed US paleontologists to remove delicate dinosaur teeth from hard sandstone.

The study of excavated fossils has also become easier with recent **technologies**. Today, scientists are **3-D** printing **replicas** of fossils for study. Meanwhile, the real bones are preserved somewhere safer.

But 3-D printing is allowing even more exciting opportunities. Fossils can now be scanned while still surrounded by rock. This creates a digital image of the fossil. Then, a 3-D printer turns the digital fossil into a physical one. Scientists may soon study and recreate dinosaur bones without even breaking ground!

DIG THIS!

Scientists hope to someday use narrow beams of light to cut through rock and reach fossils. However, further advancements are needed before these light beams can be safely used for excavation.

Paleontologists use bright lights and magnifying glasses when using air scribes. Excavators must clearly see fossil edges to avoid damaging the bones.

BONE
DIGGERS

Advanced tools have solved many problems that paleontologists face in fossil excavation and study. But some problems cannot be easily fixed by **technology**. One problem is occurring in Liaoning, where Sinosauropteryx was discovered in 1996.

Since that discovery, thousands of "bone diggers" have flooded the region. This is a name given to people who are not scientists and who dig for dinosaur fossils for profit. Bone diggers sell their finds to fossil dealers, who then sell the fossils to collectors.

This trade is illegal. However, museums and other research institutions often purchase fossils found by bone diggers. This is because these organizations do not want fossils to be locked away in private collections. Researchers purchase the fossils so they can study them.

Bone diggers have found most of the fossils displayed in museums in China. These purchases have helped encourage the illegal trade of fossils. They have also presented issues of **authenticity**.

Bone diggers can get more money by selling full skeletons. To do this, they sometimes craft fake skeletons out of fossils from different individuals or species.

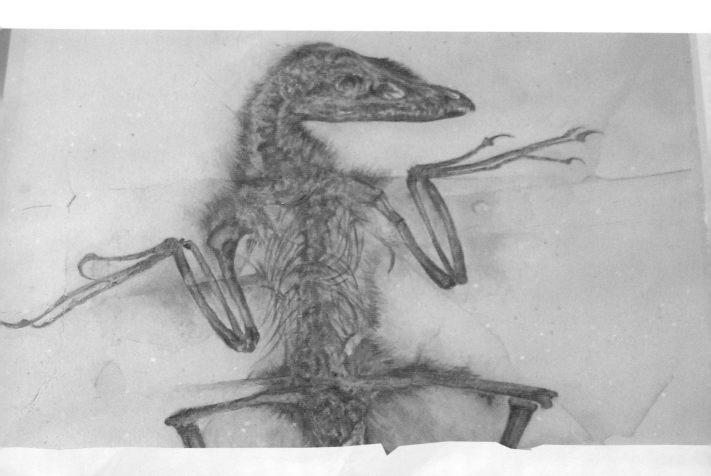

Liaoning, China, has become famous for its abundance of fossils from birdlike dinosaurs, including *Sinornithosaurus*.

This fossil forgery can even fool scientists. In 1999, paleontologists at *National Geographic* magazine announced the discovery of a new dinosaur species. Weeks later, the skeleton they used as evidence of this species was proven fake. It had come from a bone digger in Liaoning. The bone digger had pieced together fossils from two different species to make one skeleton!

Even when bone diggers present **authentic** fossils, problems may arise. Important scientific information is lost when a fossil is not excavated by a scientist. For example, scientists note the location and rock layers from which a fossil is unearthed. Bone diggers do not track this information. And without it, scientists cannot determine how old a fossil is.

Today, experts are more cautious about fossil authenticity. They are also better equipped to identify fake fossils using scanning **technologies**. Meanwhile, paleontologists continue digging for more dinosaur fossils. There is still much to uncover from the age of dinosaurs!

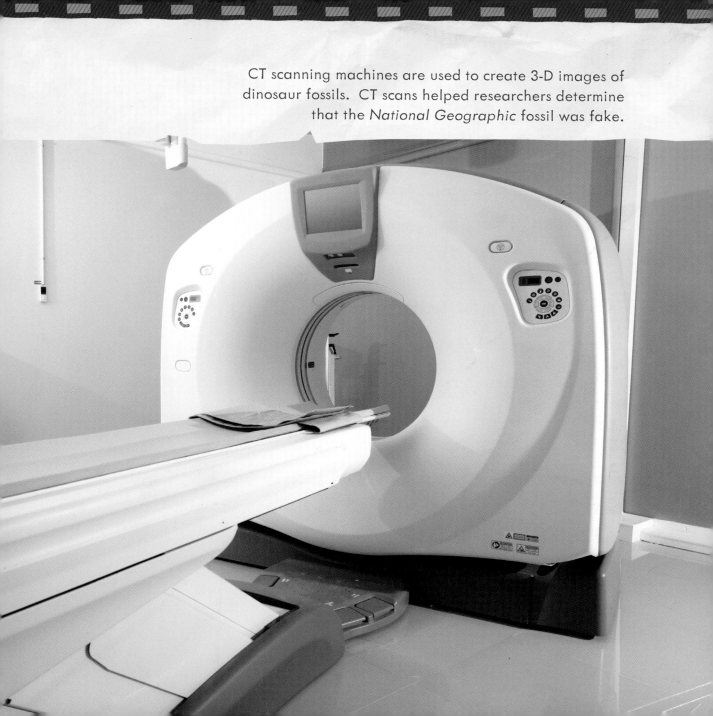

CT scanning machines are used to create 3-D images of dinosaur fossils. CT scans helped researchers determine that the *National Geographic* fossil was fake.

GLOSSARY

authenticity — the quality of being real. Something with authenticity is authentic.

classify — to arrange in groups or classes.

controversial — causing controversy. Controversy is discussion marked by strongly different views.

CT scan — a 3-D image of an object's structure created by a combination of X-ray images.

curator — a person in charge of the items on display at a museum.

evolve — to develop gradually. Evolution is the process of gradual development.

quarry — a place where stone is cut or blasted out for use in building.

radiation — the act or process of giving out light, heat, electricity, or other radiant energy.

radioactive — of, caused by, or showing radioactivity. Radioactivity is the giving off of rays of energy or particles by the breaking apart of atoms of certain elements.

replica — an exact copy.

technology (tehk-NAH-luh-jee) — a machine or piece of equipment created using science and engineering, and made to do certain tasks.

3-D — having length, width, and height. "3-D" stands for *three-dimensional*.

X-ray — an invisible and powerful light wave that can pass through solid objects.

ONLINE RESOURCES

Booklinks
NONFICTION
NETWORK
FREE! ONLINE NONFICTION RESOURCES

To learn more about dinosaur fossils, visit **abdobooklinks.com**. These links are routinely monitored and updated to provide the most current information available.

INDEX